FROM LEADS TO LOVERS THROUGH ACCOUNT-BASED MARKETING

Transforming Connections into Guaranteed Sales

Chirag Kapadia

CONTENTS

PROLOGUE

A Brighter Spark, Not a Scattered Flame !

Imagine this: you stand in a crowded marketplace, torches flickering around you. Each flame, a potential customer, lost in a sea of light. Your own torch, held high, struggles to be seen. Account-Based Marketing (ABM) is about turning that flickering flame into a beacon.

No more throwing sparks into the darkness and hoping something sticks. This is about finding the right kindling, understanding the unique needs of your most valued customers.

Forget shouting across the crowd. We'll whisper in the right ears, tailoring our message to resonate like a secret melody. This isn't about quick deals, but building bridges of trust, strong enough to weather any storm.

Ready to step out of the shadows and into the spotlight? Turn the page and let's ignite your marketing spark. We'll make you more than a flickering flame, we'll make you a guiding light.

Are you ready to shine?

CHAPTER 1: INTRODUCTION TO ACCOUNT-BASED MARKETING

I magine marketing as a giant slingshot. You load it with carefully crafted messages and launch them into the vast unknown, hoping they'll land somewhere useful. That's how marketing often feels: like throwing things at the wall and hoping something sticks.

But what if there was a better way? What if you could aim your message with precision, like a laser pointer, and focus on specific targets? This, my friend, is the magic of Account-Based Marketing (ABM).

Think of ABM as personalized marketing on steroids. Instead of throwing out generic messages to everyone, you focus all your energy on specific, high-value accounts. You get to know these accounts inside and out, tailor your message to their unique needs, and watch them blossom into loyal customers.

It's like having a dedicated team of marketing experts working on each of your most important accounts. They're constantly researching, strategizing, and crafting campaigns that are guaranteed to resonate. No more wasted time or resources on the wrong audience.

ABM is about building relationships, not just casting a wide net. It's about understanding your target accounts, addressing their specific challenges, and demonstrating how your product or service can be the perfect solution. It's about creating win-win partnerships that last.

Ready to trade the slingshot for the laser pointer? Then join me on this journey into the world of Account-Based Marketing. We'll explore the basics, uncover the secrets, and unlock the power of this transformative approach. It's time to stop throwing spaghetti at the wall and start aiming for the bull's-eye!

1.1 Understanding the Basics of Account-Based Marketing: A Deep Dive into Targeted Growth

Imagine a world where your marketing efforts are laser-focused, like a skilled sniper aiming for a single, high-value target. This is the world of Account-Based Marketing (ABM), a strategy that has revolutionized the B2B landscape, moving away from the scattergun approach of traditional marketing and towards a highly targeted and personalized approach.

ABM is not just a marketing tactic; it's a transformational way of thinking about customer acquisition and retention. It's about shifting your focus from broad audiences to specific, high-value accounts, crafting personalized campaigns that resonate with their unique needs and challenges.

The Paradigm Shift: Precision Over Volume

ABM operates on the fundamental premise of quality over quantity. Unlike traditional marketing approaches that aim to cast a wide net, hoping to capture leads in bulk, ABM takes a surgical approach. It's the art of identifying and focusing on specific high-value accounts, tailoring marketing efforts uniquely to each entity.

Targeting the Right Accounts

Imagine having a dartboard where every bullseye represents a potential client or customer. ABM equips marketers with the ability to identify these prized bullseyes. Through meticulous research, data analysis, and a deep understanding of the ideal customer profile, ABM identifies the accounts most likely to yield significant returns.

Personalization Redefined

Personalization in marketing isn't just about addressing an email with a recipient's first name. In the realm of ABM, personalization means crafting bespoke campaigns and content tailored to address the specific pain points, needs, and aspirations of each targeted account. It's about resonating with the audience on an individual level, forging a connection that transcends generic marketing noise.

Integrated Approach and Team Collaboration

ABM isn't a one-person show; it's a symphony that requires the harmonious collaboration of various departments within an organization. Sales, marketing, customer success—everyone's involved. The alignment of these teams ensures a seamless, consistent experience for the targeted accounts throughout their journey.

Measuring Success Differently

In the world of ABM, success metrics shift. It's not just about the number of leads generated; it's about the quality of engagement, the depth of relationships built, and, most importantly, the tangible impact on the bottom line. Metrics focus on account-specific ROI, conversions, and the progression of targeted accounts through the sales pipeline.

Iterative and Adaptive Approach

Flexibility is key in ABM. Marketers continuously refine strategies based on data insights and changing market dynamics. It's an iterative process that evolves as relationships with targeted accounts grow and mature.

Delving into the core principles of ABM is crucial for reaping its full potential. Let's explore each fundamental aspect in greater detail, unveiling the secrets to targeted growth:

1. Identifying Your Ideal Customer Profile (ICP)

Before embarking on your ABM journey, you need to define your blueprint : your Ideal Customer Profile (ICP). It's a crucial concept within the realm of business, marketing, and sales strategy that refers to the detailed description of the type of customer or client that a company ideally wants to target and serve. The ICP is a well-defined archetype or persona that represents the perfect fit for a business's products or services.

Here's a breakdown of the elements that typically comprise an Ideal Customer Profile:

Demographics: This includes characteristics such as age, gender, income level, geographic location, industry, company size (for B2B), and any other quantifiable data that helps in identifying the ideal customer.

Behavioral Traits: Understanding the behavioral patterns of the ideal customer is crucial. It involves analyzing how they interact with products/services, their purchasing behavior, their preferred communication channels, and any specific habits that influence their decision-making.

Challenges and Pain Points: Knowing the challenges, pain points, and problems faced by the ideal customer allows a business to tailor its products or services to directly address these issues. Understanding what keeps the ideal customer up at night helps in crafting solutions that truly resonate.

Goals and Aspirations: Understanding the goals and aspirations of the ideal customer helps in aligning a company's offerings with what the customer seeks to achieve. It's about being in sync with their desires and motivations.

Value Proposition Alignment: An ICP also involves ensuring that the value proposition of a business aligns perfectly with what the ideal customer seeks. This alignment forms the basis for effective marketing, sales, and product development strategies.

Example:

Imagine you're a software company offering a cloud-based business intelligence solution. Your ICP might be a mid-sized manufacturing company experiencing challenges with data analysis and reporting. Their ideal customer persona could be the Chief Financial Officer seeking to improve financial visibility and gain data-driven insights for better decision-making.

2. Mapping the Decision-Making Unit (DMU):

In the complex world of B2B, purchase decisions rarely rest with one individual. A group of stakeholders known as the Decision-Making Unit (DMU) collaborates and weighs in on the final decision.

Understanding the DMU is crucial for:

Personalized communication: Tailor your messaging and content to resonate with each stakeholder's specific needs and priorities.

Building relationships: Foster connections with key decision influencers.

Accelerate sales cycle: Streamline the buying process by engaging with all stakeholders involved in the decision.

Here's how to navigate the DMU landscape:

Research account structure: Identify key departments, roles, and individuals involved in the purchase process.

Analyze stakeholder influence: Assess each stakeholder's decision-making power and their influence on the final outcome.

Create a stakeholder map: Visually represent the relationships between stakeholders and their level of influence.

Develop targeted messaging: Tailor your communication to address the specific concerns and priorities of each stakeholder.

> Example:
>
> For a cloud-based BI solution, the DMU might include the CFO, Head of IT, and key department heads who rely on data-driven insights. By understanding their individual roles, concerns, and preferences, you can tailor your communication accordingly, addressing the CFO's financial concerns, the Head of IT's security considerations, and the department heads' specific data needs.

3. Orchestrating a Multi-Channel Approach:

ABM isn't about shouting your message from the rooftops. It's about orchestrating a symphony across various channels, each playing its part in captivating your target accounts. Think of each channel as an instrument in your orchestra.

Email: Your personalized emails can deliver targeted content, offers, and invitations to events.

Social media: Engage directly with key stakeholders, share valuable industry insights, and build relationships.

Events: Host exclusive events or sponsor relevant industry conferences to connect with decision-makers face-to-face.

Direct mail: Send personalized brochures, handwritten notes, or other tangible materials to make a lasting impression.

By integrating these channels seamlessly, you can create a consistent and engaging experience that guides your target accounts through the sales funnel.

4. Measuring and Adapting:

Data is the lifeblood of ABM. Just like a skilled navigator needs a compass, ABM practitioners need data to measure progress and ensure they're on the right track.

Here are some key metrics to track:

Engagement rates: How many accounts are opening your emails, visiting your website, or attending your events?

Website traffic: Are you attracting qualified leads from your target accounts?

Lead generation: How many leads are you converting from your target accounts?

Sales pipeline progression: Are leads from your target accounts moving through the sales pipeline efficiently?

Customer lifetime value: How much revenue are you generating from your target accounts?

By regularly tracking and analyzing these metrics, you can identify areas for improvement and adapt your ABM strategy accordingly. Remember, ABM is a continuous process of learning and refinement, and data is your key to success.

5. Aligning Sales and Marketing:

In the world of ABM, silos are the enemy. Sales and marketing teams need to work together seamlessly to achieve optimal results.

Imagine sales and marketing as two oars propelling a boat towards the same destination.

Sales: Provides valuable insights into customer needs, identifies key decision-makers, and closes deals.

Marketing: Creates targeted campaigns, generates qualified leads, and nurtures relationships with potential customers.

By sharing data, collaborating on strategies, and aligning their efforts, sales and marketing can create a powerful force that drives revenue and growth for the organization.

1.2 Evolution of Marketing Strategies

Imagine you're a chef who wants people to love your food. You used to shout about it to everyone on the street, hoping someone would listen. Now, you personalize your dishes to each person, even remembering their favourite ingredients! That's the evolution of marketing. It's gone from general shouts to personalized experiences, aiming to hit the bullseye of each customer's desires.

Here's a glimpse into this fascinating journey:

1. The Early Days: Shouting on the Street Corner (1800s-1940s):

Imagine a chef yelling about his amazing stew to everyone passing by. The focus was simply creating enough food and convincing people to buy it. Tools like print advertising and radio were the primary ingredients of this marketing recipe.

2. Understanding Your Taste Buds (1940s-1970s):

A wiser chef would start asking customers what they liked, what flavours they craved. Market research became the key ingredient, and the 4 Ps of marketing (product, price, place, promotion) were the spices that added flavour.

3. Building a Long-Term Relationship with Food (1970s-1990s):

The focus shifted from a single meal to creating a loyal customer base. Imagine a chef remembering your favourite dish and offering you a special welcome every time you visit. Customer satisfaction programs and brand communities became the secret ingredients for long-lasting relationships.

4. Embracing the Culinary Technology (1990s-present):

The chef enters the digital kitchen, utilizing advanced tools like websites, social media, and email. Data-driven insights became the spice that added depth and personalization to the marketing recipe.

5. The Age of Personalized Gastronomy (present and beyond):

Now, the chef prepares a unique dish for each customer, tailoring the flavours and ingredients to their individual preferences. AI and advanced analytics are the tools that enable this hyper-personalization, ensuring every experience hits the bullseye of customer desires.

Adding ABM to the Menu:

This evolution of marketing strategies is mirrored by the rise of Account-Based Marketing (ABM). Imagine the chef dedicating their time and resources to prepare a breathtakingly personalized dish for a specific VIP guest. ABM is the sniper rifle of marketing, targeting high-value accounts with laser focus and tailored strategies.

Conclusion:

Just like the chef who transitioned from shouting to serving, marketing has become more precise and customer-centric. Understanding this fascinating evolution is crucial for businesses to thrive in today's competitive landscape. So, ditch the megaphone and embrace the personalization tools available. Your customers deserve a Michelin-star experience!

CHAPTER 2: NURTURING LEADS: BUILDING THE FOUNDATION

Welcome to the second chapter of our journey into the world of Account-Based Marketing (ABM). In this chapter, we delve deeper into the practical aspects of ABM, focusing on nurturing leads and establishing a strong foundation for successful campaigns.

2.1 Identifying and Nurturing Leads

In ABM, identifying the right leads is paramount. It involves pinpointing key accounts that align with your ideal customer profile (ICP). Once identified, nurturing these leads is like tending to a garden—you need to cultivate relationships and foster engagement.

Example:

Consider an enterprise-level cybersecurity firm targeting financial institutions. They identify a major bank as a high-value account due to its need for robust security solutions. Rather than sending generic marketing materials, they craft personalized content addressing the bank's specific security concerns, providing insights into the latest threats and tailored solutions to mitigate risks.

2.2 The Power of Personalization

Personalization is a cornerstone of successful ABM strategies. It goes beyond addressing leads by name; it's about crafting tailored experiences and content that resonate with the unique needs and pain points of individual accounts.

Example:

An advertising agency focusing on automotive manufacturers personalizes its approach by creating case studies showcasing successful campaigns specifically tailored for the automotive industry. Additionally, they develop targeted ad creatives highlighting the challenges faced by these manufacturers and how their agency's expertise can address those challenges.

2.3 Embracing Multi-Channel Engagement

In the digital age, leveraging multiple communication channels is crucial in ABM. Engaging with prospects through various touchpoints such as emails, social media, webinars, direct mail, and personalized interactions helps reinforce your message and increase visibility.

Example:

An AI-driven analytics platform targeting retail chains adopts a multi-channel approach. They use targeted social media ads to reach decision-makers, conduct personalized email campaigns offering exclusive demos, and host webinars showcasing the platform's potential to revolutionize retail analytics.

2.4 Measuring Success and Adaptation

Measuring the success of ABM campaigns goes beyond lead tracking; it involves understanding the impact on revenue, ROI, and overall business growth. Continuous monitoring and analysis of campaign performance data enable agile adaptations for optimal results.

Example:

A healthcare technology company measures success by not only tracking engagement metrics but also analyzing the impact of their solutions on the efficiency of hospitals or clinics. They collect feedback from clients on how their technology has improved patient care and operational efficiency, allowing them to fine-tune their offerings to better meet the healthcare industry's evolving needs.

2.5 Real-time Process Examples:

Instead of generic emails: Imagine sending a targeted email to Mr.Sam at Star Inc., highlighting how your software solves their specific pain points in manufacturing.

Instead of mass webinars: Host a virtual event specifically for executives at your target accounts, featuring industry experts and addressing their **unique challenges.**

Instead of generic social media content: Create personalized LinkedIn posts addressing specific questions or interests of key decision-makers at target accounts.

A lead nurturing flow table can be a valuable visual representation of the stages involved in nurturing leads in an Account-Based Marketing (ABM) strategy.

Here's an example of a lead nurturing flow table outlining the typical stages and actions:

Stage	Action	Description
1. Identify	Define Ideal Customer Profile (ICP) and key accounts	Research and identify the characteristics of your ideal customers. Pinpoint high-value accounts that align with your ICP.
2. Engage	Personalized outreach	Craft tailored content and messages based on the specific needs and pain points of targeted accounts. Initiate contact through various channels like emails, social media, and events.
3. Educate	Provide valuable content	Share informative content (e.g., case studies, whitepapers, webinars) addressing challenges and solutions relevant to the targeted accounts. Educate prospects about your offerings.
4. Convert	Offer solutions and demos	Present solutions tailored to their needs. Provide product demos, trials, or consultations to showcase the value your offerings bring to their specific challenges.

Stage	Action	Description
5. Close	Sales engagement	Collaborate closely with the sales team to facilitate personalized interactions, address any remaining concerns, negotiate terms, and finalize the deal.
6. Delight	Post-sales support and nurturing	Provide exceptional post-sales support, ensuring a smooth on boarding process. Continue engaging and nurturing the relationship to foster loyalty and encourage referrals or upselling opportunities.

This table outlines a basic lead nurturing flow with sequential stages from initial identification to post-sales nurturing. Each stage involves specific actions aimed at moving the lead through the sales funnel while maintaining a personalized and tailored approach.

Customization of these stages and actions can be done based on the specific needs, industry, and strategies employed by a particular company implementing ABM. This flow table serves as a guide to create a structured process for nurturing leads effectively within an ABM framework.

Conclusion

Nurturing leads and establishing a robust foundation are fundamental in ABM. By focusing on understanding your ideal customers deeply, engaging them through personalized strategies across diverse communication channels, and adapting your approach based on measurable insights, you set the stage for sustainable business growth and long-term relationships. **Remember, ABM is about creating connections, not just collecting leads.**

CHAPTER 3: CRAFTING COMPELLING CONTENT

In our previous chapters, we've laid the foundation for lead nurturing and building the ABM framework. Now, let's dive into the heart of the matter: crafting compelling content for your target accounts. Because in this game, content is king (or queen), and it's the key to unlocking those high-value deals.

3.1 Tailoring Content for Specific Accounts

Let's face it, a one-size-fits-all approach doesn't cut it in ABM. We need to tailor our content like a bespoke suit, ensuring it fits the unique needs and interests of each target account. Here's my framework:

1. Deep Dive into Your Targets:

Research and understand your target accounts: Analyze their industry, business goals, challenges, and pain points.

Identify key decision-makers: Research their roles, responsibilities, and online presence.

Map buyer personas: Create detailed profiles for each persona, outlining their needs, priorities, and preferred communication channels.

2. Content Mapping:

Align your content with the buyer journey: Create content that addresses each stage of the journey, from awareness to decision-making.

Develop targeted content formats: Use a mix of formats like ebooks, case studies, blog posts, videos, and infographics to cater to different learning styles.

Personalize your content: Address the target account and individual decision-makers by name, reference their specific challenges, and showcase solutions tailored to their needs.

Example:

Imagine you're targeting a healthcare company struggling with patient engagement. Instead of a generic ebook on "Improving Patient Engagement," you create a personalized report titled "Boosting Patient Engagement for [Target Company Name]: Customized Strategies for Your Unique Challenges." This report highlights specific data and insights relevant to their organization, increasing their engagement and demonstrating your understanding of their needs.

3.2 Leveraging Personalization Techniques

Personalization is the magic ingredient that elevates your content from ordinary to extraordinary. Here are some techniques to sprinkle some magic into your ABM mix:

Dynamic content: Use technology to personalize content based on the individual's browsing behaviour or interests.

Interactive content: Create quizzes, polls, or interactive infographics to engage your audience and collect valuable data.

Personalized messaging: Address the individual by name, reference their past interactions, and offer relevant resources or recommendations.

Video testimonials: Showcase success stories from similar companies to build trust and credibility.

Targeted social media campaigns: Run personalized ad campaigns on LinkedIn or other platforms to reach key decision-makers directly.

Example:

Instead of a generic email blast, imagine sending a personalized video message to the CEO of a target account. In the video, you acknowledge his recent interview discussing their marketing challenges, offer a solution tailored to his specific needs, and invite him for a personalized demo. This personalized approach is far more likely to capture his attention and spark his interest.

3.3 Maximizing Engagement Through Content

Content is only half the battle; we need to ensure its engaging and resonates with our target audience. Here are some tips:

Focus on storytelling: Use narratives and case studies to connect with your audience on an emotional level.

Offer valuable insights: Share data-driven research, industry trends, and expert opinions to establish yourself as a thought leader.

Create interactive experiences: Encourage participation through quizzes, polls, and webinars to keep your audience engaged.

Optimize for different devices: Ensure your content is mobile-friendly and accessible across various platforms.

Promote your content strategically: Share your content on social media, industry platforms, and through targeted email campaigns.

Example:

Instead of a static whitepaper, imagine creating a dynamic infographic that allows users to filter data based on their specific industry or challenges. This interactive experience is more engaging and provides users with personalized insights relevant to their needs.

Remember, crafting compelling content is an ongoing process. Test, refine, and iterate your approach based on data and feedback. Be bold, be creative, and most importantly, be personal. By following these strategies, you can create content that cuts through the noise, captures attention, and ultimately drives success for your ABM program.

CHAPTER 4: ORCHESTRATING ACCOUNT-CENTRIC CAMPAIGNS

W e've explored the art of crafting captivating content, and now it's time to orchestrate those elements into campaigns that resonate with your target accounts. Think of it as conducting a symphony, where each element plays a crucial role in creating a masterpiece.

4.1 Designing Campaigns for Targeted Accounts

1. Define Campaign Objectives:

What do you want to achieve with this campaign? Increase brand awareness? Drive lead generation? Nurture existing relationships?

Align your objectives to the buyer journey stages and target account needs.

2. Develop a Compelling Narrative:

Craft a story that resonates with your target audience, highlighting their challenges and showcasing how your solutions can help. Use data, case studies, and testimonials to add credibility and impact.

Example:

Imagine you're targeting a tech company struggling with outdated software. Your campaign narrative could focus on how their competitors are leveraging new technologies to gain an edge, highlighting the negative consequences of inaction. You could then showcase your modern software solutions as the key to driving innovation and success.

3. Choose the Right Channels:

Utilize a multi-channel approach to reach your target audience where they are.

Consider email, social media, website personalization, direct mail, webinars, and events.

Tailor your channel selection to each target account and individual buyer persona.

Process Flow:

1. Target Account Selection: Identify and prioritize your key target accounts.

2. Buyer Persona Mapping: Develop detailed buyer personas for each decision-maker within the target account.

3. Campaign Objective Definition: Define specific and measurable goals for your campaign.

4. Channel Selection: Choose the most effective channels to reach your target audience and individual personas.

5. Content Creation: Develop personalized and engaging content tailored to the campaign narrative and target audience.

6. Campaign Execution: Launch your campaign across chosen channels and optimize based on performance data.

7. Measurement and Analysis: Track campaign results, measure ROI, and identify areas for improvement.

Utilizing Multi-Channel Approach

1. Email Marketing:

Use email automation to deliver personalized messages based on individual preferences and engagement levels.

Segment your audience and tailor messaging to specific buyer personas.

Include calls to action to drive engagement and conversions.

2. Social Media:

Run targeted social media campaigns to reach key decision-makers.

Utilize social listening tools to identify relevant conversations and engage with your audience.

Share valuable content that showcases your expertise and thought leadership.

3. Website Personalization:

Customize your website content and messaging based on individual visitor information.

Use retargeting campaigns to keep your brand top-of-mind.

Offer personalized recommendations and resources.

4. Direct Mail:

Use direct mail to send personalized materials like brochures, postcards, or handwritten notes.

Target high-value individuals within your target accounts.

Include compelling offers and calls to action.

5. Events and Webinars:

Host industry events or webinars to attract and engage your target audience.

Invite key decision-makers and industry experts to participate.

Share valuable insights and showcase your solutions to their challenges.

4.2 Implementing Personalized Touchpoints

1. Personalized Landing Pages:

Create customized landing pages for each target account, highlighting their specific needs and challenges.

Offer relevant content and resources tailored to their interests.

Include calls to action that drive them further down the sales funnel.

2. Account-Based Advertising:

Run targeted advertising campaigns on platforms like LinkedIn to reach specific individuals within your target accounts.

Use dynamic creatives that personalize messaging based on individual profiles and interests.

Track campaign results and measure ROI to optimize your approach.

3. Executive Engagement Programs:

Develop personalized outreach programs for key decision-makers within your target accounts.

Offer tailored content, demos, and meetings tailored to their specific needs.

Build relationships and establish yourself as a trusted advisor.

Remember, ABM is all about building relationships and creating personalized experiences. By orchestrating account-centric campaigns that utilize a multi-channel approach and incorporate personalized touchpoints, you can effectively engage your target accounts and drive successful outcomes for your ABM program.

CHAPTER 5: THE ROLE OF DATA IN ABM SUCCESS

W e've explored content creation, campaign orchestration, and personalized touchpoints. Now, let's delve into the lifeblood of ABM – data. Think of it as the fuel powering your ABM engine, driving informed decisions and propelling you towards success.

You know I'm all about crafting killer content and orchestrating campaigns that leave your target accounts breathless. But without the right data, it's like steering a ship blindfolded in a storm. So, let's dive deep into the data ocean and discover the secrets to ABM success.

5.1: Harnessing Data for Effective Targeting

Think of your ICPs as the hottest clubs in town. You wouldn't just crash any door, would you? You'd need the right intel, the VIP pass. Data is that pass, allowing you to identify and prioritize the accounts that are the perfect fit for your business. It's like having a map to hidden treasure, leading you straight to the companies with the biggest potential.

Here's my expert tip: Don't just collect data, curate it. Analyze website traffic, social media activity, industry publications – become a data detective and uncover the secrets of your target accounts. It's like eavesdropping on their conversations, learning their deepest desires and biggest challenges. This knowledge is your power, allowing you to tailor your approach and become their knight in shining armor.

5.2: Analysing and Utilizing Insights

Data is like a treasure chest overflowing with gold coins, but they're useless if you don't know how to spend them. You need to analyze the data, extract those juicy insights, and turn them into actionable strategies. Imagine being able to predict the future – data empowers you to do just that. You can identify trends, understand buyer behavior, and see what's coming down the road before your competitors even have a clue.

Listen up, ABM champions: Don't become a data hoarder. Use those insights to optimize your campaigns like a master chef. Imagine crafting content that resonates so deeply, it leaves your target accounts speechless. Imagine delivering personalized experiences so perfectly tailored, they feel like you're reading their minds. That's the power of data-driven insights, and it's the key to unlocking ABM success.

5.3: Ensuring Data Privacy and Compliance

Let's be honest, data can be a slippery fish. It's powerful, but it needs to be handled with care. We all know the horror stories of data breaches and privacy scandals. That's why compliance is non-negotiable. You need to be like a ninja, operating in the shadows, collecting and using data ethically and responsibly.

Step Table: Leveraging Data for ABM Success

Step	Description
Data Collection	Gather information from various sources: CRM data, web analytics, intent data, and

	more.
Data Analysis	Analyze and segment data to identify trends, patterns, and account-specific insights.
Personalizatio n	Utilize data insights to personalize content, messaging, and campaigns for targeted accounts.
Targeted Outreach	Implement targeted outreach based on data-driven insights, engaging prospects through preferred channels.
Measurement	Continuously measure and analyze campaign performance using data to optimize strategies.

Remember, my friends: Respect is key. Get consent before collecting data, be transparent about how you use it, and protect it like your most valuable asset. It's like building trust with your target audience. Show them you care about their privacy, and they'll reward you with their loyalty and engagement.

So, dive headfirst into the data ocean, ABM warriors! Ride the wave of insights, target your campaigns like a laser, and unlock the incredible power of data-driven ABM.

Remember, the future belongs to those who can harness the data deluge and navigate its currents with wisdom and responsibility.

CHAPTER 6: CONVERTING LEADS INTO LOYAL CUSTOMERS

We've built bridges of connection, nurtured relationships, and earned trust with our leads. Now, it's time to cross the finish line and convert those leads into loyal customers. Think of it as reaching the peak of a mountain, the culmination of your ABM journey.

6.1 Implementing Conversion Strategies

Imagine your sales funnel as a rollercoaster ride. You want your leads to smoothly navigate through each stage, ultimately reaching the exhilarating climax – becoming loyal customers. To achieve this, you need effective conversion strategies:

Steps Table : Process Flow

Stage	Action	Example
Lead Scoring	Analyze website behaviour, email engagement, and content preferences.	Assign scores based on engagement level: High, Medium, and Low.
Content Personalizati on	Create personalized landing pages, email campaigns, and social media content.	Tailor content to address specific challenges and interests.
Lead Nurturing	Send personalized emails, offer downloadable guides, and invite	Provide value and build trust through engaging content.

	them to webinars.	
Sales Engagement	Initiate calls, schedule meetings, and follow up with qualified leads.	Address specific needs and offer tailored solutions.
Offer Management	Present customized proposals and address any concerns or objections.	Highlight the value proposition and demonstrate ROI.
Customer On boarding	Provide training resources, offer ongoing support, and request feedback.	Ensure a smooth transition and build long-term relationships.

My Expert Tip: Don't just push leads down the funnel – guide them gently. Be there for them at every step of the journey, addressing their questions and concerns. Remember, conversion is not a one-time event, it's an ongoing process of building trust and nurturing relationships.

6.2 Optimizing Sales Funnels

Think of your sales funnel as a living organism, constantly evolving and adapting to the changing landscape. Regularly analyse data, identify bottlenecks, and test different strategies to optimize its performance.

Here are some optimization tips:

- A/B test your landing pages and calls to action.
- Personalize your email campaigns based on lead

behaviour.

- Track conversion rates at each stage of the funnel.
- Identify and address any friction points that hinder conversion.
- Refine your targeting criteria to attract more qualified leads.

Remember: Optimization is an ongoing process. Never stop learning, adapting, and improving your sales funnel.

6.3 Measuring Success and ROI

ABM is all about driving results, so measurement is crucial. Track key metrics like lead generation, conversion rates, customer lifetime value, and ROI. This data will help you evaluate the effectiveness of your ABM program and demonstrate its value to stakeholders.

Here are some key metrics to track:

Lead generation rate: The number of leads generated from your ABM efforts.

Conversion rate: The percentage of leads that convert into customers.

Customer lifetime value: The total revenue generated by a customer over their lifetime.

ROI: The return on investment for your ABM program.

By regularly measuring your success, you can identify areas for improvement, optimize your campaigns, and demonstrate the true value of your ABM program.

Here's an additional example to illustrate the conversion process:

Imagine you're targeting a software company looking for a new CRM solution. You implement the following strategies:

Lead Scoring: You score website visitors based on their browsing behavior and content downloads. High-scoring leads are considered more qualified and prioritized for sales outreach.

Content Personalization: You create case studies showcasing successful CRM implementations in similar companies. You also personalize email campaigns with the target company's name and highlight how your solution addresses their specific challenges.

Lead Nurturing: You invite the target company to a webinar on best practices for selecting a CRM solution. You also offer a free demo of your software.

Sales Engagement: A qualified salesperson initiates a call with the target company to discuss their specific needs and answer any questions.

Offer Management: You present a customized proposal outlining the benefits and pricing of your CRM solution. You address any concerns and objections raised by the target company.

Customer On boarding: You provide comprehensive training and support to the target company after they purchase your software.

You build a strong relationship with the target company and become their trusted partner in CRM implementation.

By implementing these strategies, you are able to convert the target company into a loyal customer who generates significant revenue for your business. This example demonstrates how a well-defined conversion strategy can lead to success in your ABM program.

Remember: Converting leads into loyal customers is a journey, not a destination. It requires continuous effort, dedication, and a clear understanding of your target accounts. By implementing effective conversion strategies, optimizing your sales funnel, and measuring your success, you can achieve remarkable results and build a loyal customer base that fuels your brand's long-term success.

So, go forth, ABM champions, and convert those leads into loyal customers! Use the process flow, examples, and table provided in this chapter as a guide to develop and execute your own successful conversion strategies. Remember, the key to success lies in personalization, engagement, and continuous improvement. By following these principles, you can unlock the full potential of your ABM program and achieve outstanding results.

CHAPTER 7: RETENTION STRATEGIES FOR LONG-TERM RELATIONSHIP

You've scaled the mountains of lead acquisition and crossed the treacherous plains of conversion. Now, it's time to embark on a new adventure: building long-term relationships with your valued customers. Remember, in the ever-shifting landscape of business, retaining loyal customers is just as crucial as acquiring new ones. This chapter will equip you with the knowledge and strategies to nurture those relationships, ensuring your customers remain your most vocal advocates and a source of consistent growth.

The Power of Retention: Cultivating Loyalty and Recurring Revenue

Let's face it, acquiring new customers is a demanding task. It requires resources, time, and strategic effort. But the truth is, retaining existing customers offers a far more rewarding ROI. Studies reveal that a mere 5% increase in customer retention can skyrocket your profits by an astounding 25% to 95%. Think about it – loyal customers generate recurring revenue, provide valuable feedback, and become your most ardent brand ambassadors. They're the cornerstone of your success, and nurturing their loyalty is the key to unlocking long-term growth.

7.1 Post-Sale Engagement Techniques: Keeping the Spark Alive

Building lasting relationships doesn't end with the initial transaction. It's an ongoing journey that requires continuous engagement and nurturing.

Here are some potent strategies to keep your customers connected and invested:

1. Regular Communication: Don't let the conversation fade. Stay connected with your customers through personalized email campaigns, engaging newsletters, and active social media interactions. Share valuable content, industry updates, and exclusive offers to reignite their interest and keep them informed.

2. Proactive Support: Don't wait for problems to arise. Be the first to offer assistance and proactively address potential concerns. Provide live chat support, create comprehensive FAQs, and offer tutorials to empower your customers and demonstrate your commitment to their success.

3. Customer Success Programs: Go beyond mere support and forge a true partnership. Develop dedicated customer success programs designed to help your customers achieve their goals. Offer personalized guidance, tailor training resources to their specific needs, and provide access to exclusive benefits like early access to new features or priority support.

4. Event and Community Building: Foster a sense of belonging and create a vibrant ecosystem around your brand. Host events, webinars, and online forums where your customers can connect, learn, and network with each other. This not only strengthens their relationship with your brand but also fosters a sense of community and shared experience.

> Example:
>
> Imagine you're a financial services provider. After a client opens an account, you send them a personalized welcome email with helpful tips on managing their finances. You also invite them to join your online forum where they can ask questions, share experiences, and connect with other clients.

7.2 Upselling and Cross-selling: Expanding Value and Driving Growth

Once you've established a strong foundation of trust and satisfaction, you can explore opportunities to further enhance the value you offer. Upselling and cross-selling complementary products or services can be a win-win situation, providing your customers with solutions they need and generating additional revenue for your business.

Here are some key principles to guide your upselling and cross-selling efforts:

1. Deep Customer Understanding: Before suggesting anything, take the time to understand your customer's needs, challenges, and current usage patterns. Analyze their purchase history, preferences, and specific goals.

2. Relevant Recommendations: Resist the urge to push products. Instead, focus on recommending solutions that truly complement their existing setup and address their specific needs. Clearly demonstrate how these offerings can help them achieve their desired outcomes.

3. Quantified Value Proposition: Don't just talk about features;

focus on benefits. Highlight the quantifiable value proposition of upgrading or adding additional services. Show how it can save them costs, increase efficiency, or improve their results.

4. Exceptional Service: Throughout the upselling and cross-selling process, prioritize customer experience. Address concerns promptly, answer questions clearly, and make the process seamless and positive.

Example:

Imagine you're a software company and a customer is using your basic plan. You identify that they're facing challenges with data management and reporting. You offer them an upgrade to a premium plan that includes advanced data analytics tools and dedicated customer support. You clearly demonstrate how this upgrade can address their specific data challenges and help them unlock valuable insights.

7.3: Customer Advocacy and Referral Programs: Harnessing the Power of Loyalty

Your most loyal customers can become your most powerful advocates. By nurturing their enthusiasm and encouraging them to share their positive experiences, you can leverage word-of-mouth marketing to attract new clients and build trust in your brand.

Here are some ways to ignite customer advocacy:

1. Implement a Referral Program: Reward your loyal customers for referring new business by offering discounts, commissions, or exclusive benefits. This incentivizes them to share their positive experiences with their network and encourages them to become active brand ambassadors.

2. Develop a Customer Advisory Board: Assemble a group of your most engaged customers to gather valuable feedback and insights. Involve them in shaping your product roadmap, brand strategy, and future developments. This gives them a sense of ownership and empowers them to contribute to your success.

3. Showcase Customer Success Stories: Share positive testimonials, case studies, and video reviews on your website and social media platforms. Hearing from satisfied customers builds trust and credibility, demonstrating the value your brand delivers.

4. Recognize and Appreciate Your Advocates: Go the extra mile to show your appreciation for customers who go above and beyond to promote your brand. Publicly acknowledge their contributions, offer exclusive rewards or experiences, and make them feel valued and appreciated.

Example:

Imagine you have a customer who consistently recommends your products to their network and provides valuable feedback. You invite them to join your customer advisory board and offer them early access to new features and product updates. You also feature their success story on your website and highlight their contributions in social media campaigns.

7.4: Building Long-Term Relationships: The Cornerstone of ABM Success

Nurturing lasting relationships with your customers is not just a strategic choice; it's the very foundation of ABM success. **By implementing effective retention strategies, you can:**

Boost Customer Lifetime Value: Loyal customers generate recurring revenue, reducing the need for costly customer acquisition efforts.

Enhance Brand Loyalty and Advocacy: Happy customers become vocal brand ambassadors, attracting new clients and expanding your reach organically.

Gain Valuable Feedback and Insights: Regularly engaging with your customers provides invaluable insights into their needs, challenges, and preferences, allowing you to continuously improve your products and services.

Foster Innovation and Growth: A loyal customer base provides the stability and support needed to make bold decisions, invest in innovation, and drive sustainable long-term growth.

Remember, it's not just about acquiring customers; it's about cultivating relationships that thrive over time. By investing in post-sale engagement, exploring upselling and cross-selling opportunities, and leveraging the power of customer advocacy, you can unlock the true potential of your ABM program and build a thriving community of loyal customers who drive your success for years to come.

So, go forth, fellow ABM warriors, and embark on this rewarding journey of nurturing long-term relationships! Implement these powerful strategies, foster a culture of loyalty and appreciation, and watch your ABM program blossom into a sustainable source of growth and prosperity. **Remember, your customers are your most valuable asset, and by nurturing those relationships,** you pave the way for a future of shared success and mutual fulfilment.

CHAPTER 8: ADDRESSING COMMON PITFALLS IN ACCOUNT-BASED MARKETING

Account-Based Marketing (ABM) offers a powerful approach to driving predictable revenue growth by focusing on high-value target accounts. However, despite its potential, ABM can face a number of challenges that can hinder its success. Recognizing and addressing these common pitfalls is crucial for maximizing the effectiveness of your program.

1. Lack of Alignment:

One of the most significant challenges to ABM success is a lack of alignment between different departments, particularly sales and marketing. Siloed thinking and miscommunication can lead to inconsistent messaging, uncoordinated outreach efforts, and ultimately, suboptimal results.

Solution:

Establish clear communication channels: Regular meetings, cross-departmental working groups, and shared dashboards can foster closer collaboration and ensure everyone is on the same page.

Define roles and responsibilities: Clearly define who is accountable for each aspect of the ABM program, avoiding duplication of effort and ensuring efficient execution.

Align goals and metrics: Set shared goals and track agreed-upon metrics to measure progress and ensure everyone is working towards the same objectives.

2. Data Silos and Fragmentation:

Fragmented data across different platforms and systems can hinder your ability to personalize your approach and gain valuable insights from your target accounts. Incomplete or inaccurate data can lead to misinformed decisions and missed opportunities.

Solution:

Invest in data integration tools: Implement tools that consolidate data from various sources, providing a unified view of your target accounts and their interactions with your brand.

Cleanse and standardize data: Regularly review and update your data to ensure its accuracy and consistency.

Utilize data analytics tools: Leverage data analytics to extract valuable insights from your data, identify trends, and inform your decision-making.

3. Siloed Thinking and Lack of Cross-functional Collaboration:

Encouraging a collaborative mindset across departments is crucial for successful ABM. Breaking down silos and fostering cross-functional collaboration can lead to a more comprehensive understanding of your target accounts and their needs, enabling you to develop more effective solutions.

Solution:

Create cross-functional teams: Establish dedicated ABM teams consisting of members from sales, marketing, and other relevant departments.

Encourage knowledge sharing: Facilitate regular communication and knowledge sharing between different teams to promote a holistic understanding of your target accounts.

Break down departmental barriers: Create a culture of collaboration and shared ownership of the ABM program.

4. Lack of Personalization:

Generic, one-size-fits-all messaging is unlikely to resonate with your target accounts. Tailor your content, communication, and outreach efforts to the specific needs, challenges, and interests of each individual decision-maker within your target accounts.

Solution:

Develop buyer personas: Create detailed profiles of your ideal customers, including their demographics, pain points, and decision-making processes.

Segment your audience: Divide your target accounts into smaller groups based on shared characteristics and tailor your outreach accordingly.

Personalize your messaging: Craft relevant content and communications that address the specific needs and interests of each individual decision-maker.

5. Measuring the Wrong Metrics:

Focusing solely on short-term metrics like lead generation tells only part of the story. It's crucial to track long-term metrics such as customer lifetime value, account penetration, and revenue growth to assess the true impact of your ABM program.

Solution:

Define a comprehensive set of metrics: Establish a clear set of metrics that align with your ABM goals and track progress over time.

Go beyond the surface: Don't just focus on vanity metrics; track metrics that provide a deeper understanding of customer engagement and program effectiveness.

Regularly analyze data and adapt your strategy: Use data insights to identify areas for improvement and adjust your approach to optimize program performance.

6. Resource Constraints:

Implementing a successful ABM program requires dedicated resources, including budget, personnel with relevant expertise, and access to necessary technology. Insufficient resources can limit the program's reach and impact.

Solution:

Invest in ABM resources: Allocate sufficient budget, recruit skilled personnel, and invest in technology tools to support your ABM program.

Prioritize key accounts: Focus your resources on the most high-value target accounts to maximize return on investment.

Seek external support: Consider partnering with agencies or consultants who can provide specialized expertise and resources.

7. Lack of Patience and Long-Term Focus:

ABM is a long-term strategy that requires sustained effort and patience to see significant results. Expecting immediate success can lead to frustration and discouragement.

Solution:

Set realistic expectations: Understand that ABM requires time to build relationships, generate trust, and drive results.

Focus on long-term metrics: Track your progress against long-term metrics like customer lifetime value and account penetration, not just short-term indicators like lead generation.

Celebrate milestones: Recognize and celebrate successes along the way to maintain motivation and momentum.

Continuously adapt and improve: Regularly review your program and make adjustments based on results and market changes.

8. Failure to Embrace Technology and Innovation:

The ABM landscape is rapidly evolving, and new technologies are constantly emerging. Failing to embrace these advancements can hinder your ability to compete effectively and deliver personalized experiences.

Solution:

Stay up-to-date on the latest trends: Actively research and learn about emerging technologies relevant to ABM.

Experiment with new technologies: Pilot new tools and platforms to see how they can enhance your program.

Invest in technology infrastructure: Ensure you have the necessary technology infrastructure in place to support your ABM efforts.

9. Ignoring the Importance of Data Governance:

Data governance is essential for ensuring the accuracy, consistency, and security of your data. Without proper data governance, your ABM program can suffer from inaccuracies, inconsistencies, and compliance issues.

Solution:

Implement data governance policies and procedures: Establish clear guidelines for data collection, storage, access, and utilization.

Invest in data quality tools: Utilize data quality tools to identify and correct errors in your data.

Regularly review and update your data governance practices: Adapt your policies and procedures to ensure they remain effective in a constantly evolving landscape.

10. Underestimating the Power of Relationship Building:

Building strong relationships with your target accounts is the foundation of successful ABM. This involves going beyond transactional interactions and focusing on genuine engagement, value creation, and trust-building.

Solution:

Develop a customer-centric approach: Focus on understanding your target accounts' needs and challenges and tailor your solutions accordingly.

Prioritize personalized interactions: Build relationships with individual decision-makers within your target accounts, not just the organization as a whole.

Provide value beyond sales: Offer valuable resources, insights, and support to your target accounts without expecting anything in return.

By recognizing and addressing these common pitfalls, you can significantly increase your chances of success with ABM.

Remember, ABM is a journey, not a destination. It requires continuous effort, adaptation, and a commitment to building lasting relationships with your target accounts. By addressing these challenges proactively, you can unlock the full potential of ABM and drive sustainable growth for your business.

CHAPTER 9: FUTURE TRENDS IN ACCOUNT-BASED MARKETING

The world of Account-Based Marketing (ABM) is constantly evolving, driven by technological advancements and shifting customer behaviour. As we navigate this dynamic landscape, staying ahead of the curve is essential for success. This chapter delves into the exciting future of ABM, exploring emerging trends, technologies, and strategies to prepare you for what lies ahead.

10.1 Predictions and Emerging Technologies

The future of ABM is brimming with possibilities, fuelled by innovative technologies and evolving customer expectations. Let's explore some key trends that will shape the ABM landscape:

Trend	Description	Impact
Hyper-personalization	Crafting individual experiences for each decision-maker	Increased engagement, stronger relationships
Predictive Analytics	Anticipating future customer needs	Proactive solutions, positioning as a trusted advisor
Account-Based Orchestration	Seamless integration of all ABM tools and platforms	Streamlined workflows, optimized resource allocation
Rise of AI and Automation	Automation of repetitive tasks	Increased efficiency, focus on high-value activities
New Era of Customer-Centricity	Personalized, omnichannel experiences	Enhanced customer satisfaction, loyalty, and advocacy

10.2 The Role of AI and Automation in ABM

AI and automation are poised to revolutionize the ABM landscape. These technologies will streamline processes, enhance personalization, and enable marketers to reach new heights of effectiveness. Here are some key applications of AI and automation in ABM:

1. Lead Scoring and Segmentation: Identify high-potential leads with greater accuracy, allowing you to focus your resources on the most promising opportunities. AI algorithms can analyze data from various sources to identify key triggers and predict conversion likelihood.

2. Content Personalization: Deliver personalized content that resonates with individual decision-makers. AI can analyze user behaviour, interests, and preferences to tailor content that addresses their specific needs and challenges.

3. Predictive Lead Nurturing: Proactively engage with leads based on their predicted behaviour. AI can identify patterns in customer behaviour and trigger targeted campaigns at the optimal time, maximizing engagement and conversion rates.

4. Automate Repetitive Tasks: Free up valuable time for strategic tasks by automating repetitive tasks like data entry, reporting, and campaign management. This allows your team to focus on creativity, relationship building, and high-impact activities.

5. Optimizing Campaign Performance: Continuously improve your ABM campaigns by leveraging AI-powered analytics. Identify areas for improvement, optimize budget allocation, and refine targeting to maximize campaign effectiveness.

Conclusion:

The future of ABM is filled with exciting possibilities. By embracing emerging technologies, adapting to evolving consumer behaviour, and leveraging the power of AI and automation, you can unlock the full potential of this powerful marketing strategy.

CHAPTER 10: IMPLEMENTING ACCOUNT-BASED MARKETING (ABM) ON LINKEDIN
A STEP-BY STEP GUIDE

A s LinkedIn becomes increasingly important for B2B marketing, mastering ABM on this platform offers a powerful strategy to reach and engage your high-value accounts. LinkedIn Account-Based Marketing (ABM) revolutionizes targeted B2B marketing strategies by enabling businesses to focus on high-value accounts with personalized and precise engagement.

Leveraging LinkedIn's expansive network of professionals, ABM on this platform involves tailoring marketing efforts to resonate with specific companies or individuals, aligning content, ads, and outreach to their unique needs and challenges.

Here's a step-by-step guide to get you started:

Step 1: Define Your Ideal Customer Profile (ICP) and Target Account List (TAL)

Identify your ideal customer: Define industry, company size, location, decision-maker roles, and other key characteristics.

Research and build your TAL: Leverage LinkedIn Sales Navigator, industry databases, and existing customer data to identify potential accounts.

Rank and prioritize: Evaluate accounts based on potential value, fit, and engagement levels.

Step 2: Leverage LinkedIn's Targeting Capabilities

Utilize Sales Navigator filters: Target specific companies, job titles, decision-makers, and even industry groups.

Combine targeting options: Create custom audiences based on various criteria for precise reach.

Run LinkedIn Ads: Utilize Sponsored Content, Dynamic Ads, and Lead Gen Forms to reach your target audience with personalized messages and offers.

Step 3: Craft Personalized Content and Messaging

- **Develop buyer personas:** Understand the needs, challenges, and interests of individual decision-makers within your target accounts.
- **Tailor your content:** Create blog posts, articles, case studies, and thought leadership pieces relevant to their specific pain points.
- **Personalize your messaging:** Use their names, company information, and relevant context to create a sense of connection and understanding.

Step 4: Engage and Build Relationships

- **Join relevant LinkedIn groups:** Participate in discussions, share valuable insights, and connect with decision-makers.
- **Engage directly:** Send personalized messages, initiate conversations, and offer helpful resources.

- **Leverage LinkedIn features:** Utilize recommendations, endorsements, and social proof to build trust and credibility.

Step 5: Track, Analyze, and Adapt

- **Monitor key metrics:** Track impressions, clicks, leads generated, website traffic, and conversions to measure campaign effectiveness.
- **Analyze data and gain insights:** Identify what's working and what needs improvement.
- **Refine your strategy:** Adapt your targeting, content, and messaging based on data and feedback.

Step 6: Partner with Influencers

- **Identify relevant industry influencers:** Choose individuals with strong connections to your target audience.
- **Collaborate on content creation:** Partner with influencers to develop valuable content that resonates with your target accounts.
- **Leverage their reach:** Utilize influencer endorsements, interviews, and joint webinars to amplify your message.

Step 7: Measure and Optimize Your ABM Efforts

- **Quantify your results:** Calculate ROI, analyze pipeline impact, and track customer acquisition costs.
- **Identify areas for improvement:** Continuously evaluate your strategy and identify areas for optimization.

- **Adapt and evolve:** Stay informed about the latest ABM trends on LinkedIn and adapt your approach accordingly.

By following these steps and leveraging LinkedIn's powerful tools and capabilities, you can effectively implement ABM on this platform, build strong relationships with your target accounts, and drive significant business growth.

Conclusion: Transforming Connections into Guaranteed Sales - How ABM Turns Leads into Loyal Champions

Account-Based Marketing (ABM) isn't just about generating leads; it's about cultivating relationships and transforming fleeting connections into guaranteed sales. By implementing the strategies outlined in this handbook, you can effectively convert your high-value leads into loyal champions who drive predictable revenue and sustainable growth for your business.

Think of ABM as the art of turning cold leads into passionate advocates. It's about building trust, demonstrating value, and exceeding expectations at every touchpoint.

Here's how ABM turns leads into loyal champions:

1. Personalized Experiences: By tailoring your messaging, content, and outreach to each individual within your target accounts, you create a sense of exclusivity and importance, fostering stronger engagement and commitment.

2. Building Deeper Relationships: ABM goes beyond transactional interactions. It's about fostering meaningful connections with decision-makers, understanding their needs, and becoming a trusted advisor. This relationship-centric approach builds loyalty and advocacy.

3. Creating Value beyond Sales: Don't focus solely on selling your product or service. Offer valuable resources, insights, and support without expecting anything in return. This demonstrates your commitment to their success, strengthening the bond and trust.

4. Aligning Sales and Marketing: When sales and marketing teams work together with a unified ABM strategy, communication is seamless, efforts are coordinated, and results are amplified. This unified approach ensures consistent messaging and a positive customer experience throughout the entire journey.

5. Measuring and Refining: ABM is a continuous process, requiring constant monitoring and improvement. By tracking key metrics and analyzing data, you can identify what's working and what needs improvement, allowing you to refine your strategy and optimize your results.

Remember, ABM is not a magic bullet. It requires dedication, patience, and a commitment to building genuine relationships. However, when implemented effectively, ABM can unlock the true potential of your sales pipeline, turning fleeting connections into guaranteed sales and loyal champions who propel your business forward.

Embrace ABM, cultivate connections, and watch your leads transform into passionate advocates who not only purchase your product but actively drive your success.

CHAPTER 11 - THE ABM REVOLUTION: FROM LEADS TO LOYAL CHAMPIONS - A STORY OF TRANSFORMATION

I magine a world where your sales pipeline isn't a leaky faucet, but a constant stream of qualified leads, eagerly awaiting your offerings. A world where your customers aren't just names on a spreadsheet, but passionate advocates singing your praises to the rooftops. This is the transformative power of Account-Based Marketing (ABM), and it's not just a pipe dream, it's a reality within reach.

Let's step into the shoes of Sarah, a marketing director at a SaaS company struggling with traditional lead generation tactics. Her inbox overflowed with generic inquiries from unqualified leads, most of whom evaporated before reaching the sales stage. Frustrated and desperate, Sarah stumbled upon the concept of ABM. Intrigued, she delved deeper, discovering a world of personalized experiences, deep customer relationships, and guaranteed sales. Sarah knew she had to try it.

With a newfound zeal, Sarah embarked on her ABM journey. She meticulously handpicked her target accounts – companies perfectly aligned with their ideal customer profile. Sarah then conducted thorough research, crafting detailed buyer personas for each key decision-maker within those accounts. Armed with this knowledge, Sarah developed a personalized ABM strategy, crafting content that resonated with the specific needs and challenges of each individual.

Imagine Sarah's delight when the response poured in. Unlike the generic inquiries she was used to, she received engaged responses, insightful questions, and genuine interest. Sarah was no longer just another salesperson; she had become a trusted advisor, offering valuable resources and building trust.

Over time, the connections Sarah nurtured transformed into powerful partnerships. The decision-makers within her target accounts became champions of her brand, actively advocating for her product within their companies. This resulted in a dramatic shift in Sarah's sales pipeline. Leads weren't just flowing in; they were converting at an unprecedented rate. Sarah had cracked the code – she had turned fleeting connections into guaranteed sales.

The success of Sarah's ABM journey wasn't just an isolated incident. Companies across diverse industries are experiencing similar transformations, reaping the rewards of a customer-centric approach.

GUARANTEED SALES FORMULA: FROM LEADS TO LOVERS!!

Step	Description	Outcome
1. Identify High-Value Accounts (HVAs):	Conduct thorough research to pinpoint ideal customers with significant potential impact.	A focused list of target accounts aligned with your ideal customer profile.
2. Craft Buyer Personas:	Develop detailed profiles for key decision-makers within your HVAs, understanding their needs, challenges, and preferences.	In-depth knowledge of your target audience, enabling personalized outreach and messaging.
3. Design Personalized Experiences:	Tailor content, communication, and outreach to resonate with individual decision-makers based on their buyer personas.	Personalized experiences that feel relevant and valuable, driving engagement and building trust.
4. Build Meaningful Relationships:	Foster genuine connections with decision-makers, going	Strong relationships built on trust, understanding, and mutual respect.

	beyond sales-focused interactions to become a trusted advisor.	
5. Offer Value Beyond Sales:	Provide valuable resources, insights, and support without expecting immediate returns, demonstrating your commitment to their success.	Deeper connections and stronger relationships, solidifying your position as a trusted partner.
6. Utilize Targeted ABM Tools:	Leverage LinkedIn Sales Navigator, Marketo ABM, Demandbase, or other platforms to optimize targeting, manage campaigns, and track results.	Increased efficiency, improved targeting, and maximized impact of your ABM efforts.
7. Track and Analyze Performanc e:	Monitor key metrics like impressions, clicks, leads, conversions, and ROI to measure campaign	Data-driven insights to refine your strategy, optimize campaigns, and continuously improve your ABM performance.

	effectiveness and identify areas for improvement.	
8. Adapt and Evolve:	Stay informed about the latest ABM trends and adapt your approach based on data and feedback.	A dynamic and evolving ABM strategy that remains effective in a constantly changing landscape.
9. Partner with Influencers:	Collaborate with industry influencers to amplify your reach, build credibility, and reach key decision-makers.	Increased brand awareness, enhanced thought leadership, and access to new audiences.
10. Measure and Refine:	Continuously measure your ABM efforts and refine your approach based on results and data-driven insights.	Sustainable and predictable growth, maximizing the value of your ABM investments.

By implementing these guaranteed sales steps and cultivating authentic connections, you can transform leads into passionate advocates, driving predictable revenue and achieving sustainable growth for your business. Remember, ABM is a journey, not a destination. It requires dedication, patience, and a commitment to building genuine relationships. Embrace the process, and witness the transformative power of ABM!

APPENDIX: TOOLS AND RESOURCES FOR EFFECTIVE ABM

Recommended Tools and Software

Tool Name	Description	Functionality
Leadfeeder	Tells you what companies visit your website, even if they never fill out a form or contact you.	Account-based retargeting, lead generation, website visitor tracking
LeadGenius	Provides high-quality data for ABM efforts through a combination of software and human research teams.	Account-based marketing data, lead generation, contact information enrichment
Datanyze	Helps marketers build and curate a list of prospects, and score leads before and after they're in the pipeline.	Lead generation, list management, lead scoring
DataFox	Allows marketers to search for companies similar to existing customer profiles, or search for companies that fit a list of specific criteria.	Prospect identification, competitive analysis, company research
Nudge	Helps marketers and salespeople keep track of leads in their pipeline and identify contacts held in common.	Lead management, relationship management, sales pipeline optimization
ZoomInfo MarketingOS	Searches by contact and company, then compiles lists of individuals to contact within each target company.	Prospect research, list building, contact information management
LinkedIn	Allows manual search for business contacts.	Prospect research, networking, lead generation
Uberflip	Executes account-specific messaging,	Content marketing, account-based execution, sales enablement

	organizes resources, syncs content strategy.	
HubSpot	Offers Smart Content feature that delivers personalized content to prospects.	Marketing automation, content management, sales enablement
Adobe Campaign	Robust tools for email and mobile marketing, campaign creation, and journey management.	Marketing automation, campaign management, customer journey analysis
Act-On	Offers ABM-specific features like dynamic content and predictive email sending.	Marketing automation, email marketing, lead scoring
PathFactory	Provides content insights and activation, tracks prospect interaction with content.	Content analytics, content personalization, content marketing
Personyze	Omnichannel personalization platform for B2B and B2C marketing.	Personalization, customer journey optimization, marketing automation
Integrate	Syncs with lead data platforms, cleans data, launches campaigns, and analyzes performance.	Data management, campaign management, analytics
Adobe Marketo Engage	Full suite of tools for ABM, including targeting, personalization, and analytics.	Marketing automation, account-based marketing, campaign management
Apollo	Provides suggestions for messaging prospects based on their activity.	Sales intelligence, prospecting, lead engagement
Vainu	Vainu is an ABM tool that helps businesses identify their ideal customers and target them with highly personalized messaging.	Has limited coverage in certain geographic regions. Has a steep learning curve. Can be expensive for small businesses or occasional lead-generation efforts
SendPulse	SendPulse offers diverse tools for small businesses, from landing pages to WhatsApp chatbots, creating an all-	All the essential marketing tools on a single platform flexible pricing model 24/7 customer support for paid users

	in-one solution for multichannel marketing.	
InsideView	InsideView's ABM tool empowers sales and marketing to identify, target, and engage ideal customers, enhancing ABM campaign effectiveness.	Account scoring prioritizes leads, predictive analytics identifies opportunities, and segmentation tools target specific accounts, optimizing marketing strategies effectively.
Alyce	Alyce's AI-driven corporate gifting platform uses ABM to provide personalized gifts, accelerating deals and reducing churn, with integrated analytics for optimization.	Expense, campaign execution issues, and resource demands may pose challenges. Evaluate cost-effectiveness and readiness before implementing this tool.
ReachDesk	Reachdesk, a cost-effective ABM tool, facilitates personalized campaigns with robust features, but businesses need to assess the learning curve and commitment.	Provides personalized gifts, integrates with marketing automation and CRM, and offers detailed analytics for measuring campaign effectiveness.
Terminus ABM Platform	Terminus, an industry leader in ABM, enhances brand awareness and targets in-market accounts with multi-channel experiences, recognized in industry reports.	Terminus excels in ABM with features like targeting, personalization, analytics, and user-friendly interfaces, offering seamless integrations and robust reporting capabilities.
LeanData	LeanData, a top ABM solution, facilitates personalized campaigns through advanced lead scoring, automation, segmentation, and robust analytics, essential for impactful strategies.	LeanData streamlines campaign setup with an easy interface, robust segmentation, automated workflows, and detailed reporting for optimizing performance over time.

Content Spectrum

VARIED TOPICS ON MARKETING, SALES, AND CUSTOMER RETENTION EXPLORED

Engaging and Informative Contributions Resonating with Diverse Audiences

As a seasoned author in the realm of Marketing and Sales within the local print media, my expertise extends beyond the confines of technology. With a wealth of experience, I have contributed extensively to both local print and digital platforms, showcasing my proficiency through the publication of over 50 insightful articles.

Impactful Insights

Furthermore, beyond the significant number of published articles, I aim to extend my influence by delving deeper into complex industry-related subjects. My writing isn't just informative; it's a catalyst for change through my consulting services.

My Articles
IN PRINT MEDIA

Over 50 Featured Articles in Local Print and Digital Media

My dedication to crafting engaging and informative content has been instrumental in fostering a deeper understanding of these vital business facets, making a tangible impact on readers within the local community and beyond.

Publication Success

These pieces cover a diverse array of subjects within the Marketing, Sales, and Customer Retention domains, delving into nuanced topics and providing valuable insights that have resonated with audiences.

Insightful Perspectives:

VARIED THEMES EXPLORED IN BUSINESS PUBLICATIONS

Delving into B2B Segment & Lead Strategies to Management

I actively engage with my audience, hosting workshops, seminars, and webinars where I share industry insights, providing mentorship to aspiring writers, marketers, and business owners.

Impactful Insights

My commitment to nurturing talent and fostering a deeper understanding of Marketing and Sales principles solidifies my role as an influential figure within the local business ecosystem.

AFTERWORD

You've reached the final page, the embers of ABM knowledge still glowing in your mind. But the journey doesn't end here. This book was just the spark, the blueprint for igniting a marketing revolution in your organization. Now, it's time to step out of the pages and into the fire.

Remember, ABM isn't just a set of tactics; it's a mindset shift. It's about seeing your customers as individuals, understanding their stories, and forging connections that go beyond the transactional. It's about building trust, not just awareness.

So, what are your next steps?
Step into the fire. Ignite your passion for ABM. And watch your marketing efforts transform from scattered sparks into a roaring inferno of success.

This book may have closed, but the story of your ABM transformation is just beginning. Remember, the future belongs to those who whisper to the right ears. Are you ready to lend them your voice?

Connect with me at www.linkedin.com/in/chiragkapadia or write me at chiragk@tactproconsulting.com and let's keep the ABM fire burning.

ACKNOWLEDGEMENT

This book wouldn't exist without the incredible tapestry of support woven by so many. To each piece, I offer my deepest gratitude:

To my family and friends: My unwavering anchor in the storm, your love and unwavering belief fueled my late nights & early mornings.

To my mentors and colleagues: Your guidance and expertise illuminated my path, and your encouragement kept my fire burning strong.

To the ABM community: You are the pioneers, the storytellers, and the unsung heroes who inspire me every day.

To my readers: Your thirst for knowledge and willingness to embark on this journey with me are the ultimate reward.

And most importantly, to the countless individuals who touched my life in ways big and small, your kindness, inspiration, and shared passion made this book a reality. Thank you.

This journey is far from over. May this book be a beacon for all who seek to transform their marketing and connect with their ideal customers in a meaningful way.

With heartfelt thanks,

Chirag Kapadia

ABOUT THE AUTHOR

Chirag Kapadia

Chirag Kapadia is a seasoned Technocrat with over 20 years of expertise in the realms of Technology, Sales, and Marketing. He's authored over 50 articles in local print media, conducted 200+ sessions on diverse industry topics, and is devoted to his pursuits as a passionate learner. With a strong inclination towards entrepreneurship, Chirag has ventured into the realm of consulting, leveraging his extensive knowledge. He's currently working on his first book, delving into subjects he's mastered. Connect with him on LinkedIn at www.linkedin.com/in/chiragkapadia to explore his insights and professional journey.

www.ingramcontent.com/pod-product-compliance
Lightning Source LLC
Chambersburg PA
CBHW072342290526
45794CB00002B/988